IMAGES
of America

FLOYD COUNTY

In this winter 1914 photograph, John B. Clark (front) and Beverley McCown, members of Elkhorn Coal Company's police force for Wayland and Garrett, ride on velocipedes near Wayland. Velocipedes such as these are pedaled, like bicycles, to move them along railroad tracks. For areas with poor roadway access, the velocipede allowed travel between towns; the attached basket made it possible to carry supplies. (Courtesy of Alice Lloyd College.)

ON THE COVER: Shifts change at the mine portal in the afternoon. Employees of Inland Steel Company's Wheelwright Nos. 1 and 2 mines prepare to go underground, where they will work for several hours undercutting coal, drilling holes, loading explosive charges, loading coal, and laying new tracks. This photograph was taken by Russell Lee on September 23, 1946. (Courtesy of the National Archives.)

IMAGES
of America

FLOYD COUNTY

Lisa Perry and the
Wheelwright Historical Society

ARCADIA
PUBLISHING

Published by Arcadia Publishing
Charleston SC, Chicago IL, Portsmouth NH, San Francisco CA

Library of Congress Control Number: 2009939979

For all general information contact Arcadia Publishing at:
Telephone 843-853-2070
Fax 843-853-0044
E-mail sales@arcadiapublishing.com
For customer service and orders:
Toll-Free 1-888-313-2665

Visit us on the Internet at www.arcadiapublishing.com

To the people of Wheelwright, past and present, who inspired my initial research in Floyd County and to all those who kept the memories alive.

CONTENTS

Acknowledgments 6

Introduction 7

1. In the Kingdom of Coal 9

2. Rail Development Opens Doors to Growth 15

3. Coal Camp Life 31

4. Community Services 45

5. Work Life 55

6. Coal Camp Baseball 75

7. Coal Camp Schools 81

8. Coal Camp Churches 93

9. Coal Camp Leisure and Entertainment 101

10. Legends and Heroes 117

Bibliography 126

About the Wheelwright Historical Society 127

ACKNOWLEDGMENTS

I would like to express my sincere appreciation to the people of Floyd County who made this book possible. These include Marionette Burgess, Mary Lamm, Josephine Martin, Scott and Douglas Scutchfield, Richard Shockley, and Edward Tucker for sharing photographs from their family albums and personal collections.

I also owe a tremendous debt of gratitude to Everett Young of the Chesapeake and Ohio Historical Society (COHS) for his tireless efforts in answering endless questions about the development of rail lines in Floyd County and for sharing the extensive collections from the archive. No other source could have provided these amazing photographs and depth of historical information. The COHS community is without peer in their dedication to the collection and preservation of regional railroad lore.

Jerry Fultz, director of the Wayland Historical Society (WHS), spent days answering questions, helping with photographic descriptions, and providing information on the development of Wayland and other nearby communities. His help in directing me to private collections in addition to those of WHS was also invaluable. The members of that organization have worked hard to provide a comprehensive collection to document development in that region of the county.

The extensive collection of Appalachian photographs at Alice Lloyd College provided thousands of pictures to choose from in the creation of this book. Their willingness to share helped provide insights into everyday life in the coal camps.

A special thank you goes to the National Archives. The collection of photographs from Wheelwright housed there served as the basis for the photographic history of that community.

A final thanks goes out to South Floyd High School, their 2008–2009 STLP students, and Wheelwright Historical Society for their support in this project. Their tireless efforts can never be repaid except in thanks and in ongoing funding for their work in preserving the heritage of the region.

And to Robert Clark, for all the technical assistance and support, all my gratitude is still not enough.

Most images in this volume appear courtesy of Alice Lloyd College (ALC), the Chesapeake and Ohio Historical Society (COHS), the National Archives (NA), and the Wayland Historical Society (WHS).

INTRODUCTION

Floyd County, named for Kentucky pioneer John Floyd, was formed by the Kentucky legislature in 1799. Originally encompassing all of the Big Sandy River Valley and much of eastern Kentucky, the boundaries included portions of what are now Pike, Martin, Knott, Magoffin, and Johnson Counties. Sections of the county were carved away in the early decades of the county so that, by 1884, it reached its current boundary encompassing nearly 400 square miles. River trade, made possible because the Levisa Fork of the Big Sandy River was navigable for much of the year, helped to establish commercial trading posts early in the county's history. Prestonsburg, the county seat, was established primarily as a commercial river trading post in the late 18th century. John Spurlock is believed to have built the first cabin in the area in 1791; the town itself was not surveyed until 1797.

Inland from the river, Floyd County has a rugged, mountainous terrain. Those who chose to live in the more remote areas of the county faced difficulties in transportation, lack of regular jobs, and few resources other than those they could find or create for themselves locally. They relied primarily on small-scale subsistence agriculture for survival. Lacking adequate flat land to develop, large-scale agricultural enterprises found further west in the state never developed. The county had many natural resources, dominant among them coal and timber, and it was those resources that eventually brought industrial investment, more people, and a new way of life that persists even today.

In the decades following the Civil War, wealthy men from Pennsylvania, New York, and other northern industrial areas began investing in mineral rights and property in Appalachia. This was as true in Floyd County as in any coal-rich mountain county in West Virginia, eastern Kentucky, western Virginia, or eastern Tennessee. Subsistence farmers, always hungry for hard cash, were happy to take the money they were offered for rights to minerals that may or may not lie below the land they farmed. By the end of the 19th century, many of these small family farms had sold their mineral rights, not knowing of the wealth that would soon be taken from under their land.

With the coming of the railroad in 1903 and the coal industry, which began booming in the 1910s and 1920s, the county rapidly grew. The industrial growth created thousands of jobs in the county, many more jobs than the local population could fill. Jobs in the timber industry, constructing railroads, and working in the mines developed rapidly in response to a national demand for these natural resources and the transportation infrastructure to move them. In response to this demand for workers, thousands of people migrated into the county. Native-born whites from around the country, European immigrants, and African Americans from southern plantations and coalfields came to Floyd County to build the railroads, build the coal camps, and mine the coal that was in huge demand to fuel northern industrial works. What had been an agrarian, white population suddenly shifted to an industrial, multi-racial, and multi-ethnic population. Alongside the Tacketts and Halls and Johnsons could now be found Wneks, Ferraris, and Bartukas. Pentecostal, Methodist, and Baptist churches were joined by Jewish synagogues and Catholic churches. In the company stores, English was joined by Czech, Italian, Greek, Hungarian, and a host of other European languages.

To make room for all these new people coming to mine coal, the coal companies began building company towns. This construction was a matter of necessity. Because much of the county—and nearly all the coal mines being developed—was in more remote areas away from settled communities along the Big Sandy River, there was no place for workers to live. Camps generally began with tents or roughly constructed wooden shacks. Further development took place as the mine progressed, with improvements to early housing and construction of additional housing, commercial structures, entertainment facilities, churches, and schools, eventually turning these camps into towns wholly owned by the coal company. Miners generally lived in company-owned houses, shopped in company-owned stores, attended company-provided churches, attended company-build schools, and played in company-owned parks. Throughout the county, you can still find towns named for owners or investors of these coal companies. In Floyd County, many family farms were abandoned as the men went to work in the coal mines for a regular wage.

The railroads and coal industry brought only short-term prosperity to the area, but they permanently changed both the economy and culture of Floyd County. One may argue that they left little behind, but that completely overlooks the diversity of the area, the rich culture created by the blending of so many different racial and ethnic backgrounds in such a compressed time, and the infrastructure that was built simply to allow for industry. This is the story of those coal camps, the people who made them, and the rich heritage of those who remain. While the area is once again lacking in widespread industry and employment for any who want to work, and while the coal towns are often just ghosts of their former selves, living in the reflected glory of better days, there is hope aplenty for the future. Efforts such as the Jenny Wiley Theater, the Mountain Arts Center, the Kentucky Opry, and the Samuel May House celebrate the rich heritage of the area while working to preserve the traditional music, arts, and crafts that reflect the contributions of the original settlers. Many of these small coal towns celebrate their heritage and traditions through annual festivals and fairs and through local efforts to preserve remaining structures from the heyday of mining. Martin's Red, White, and Blue Festival, Prestonsburg's Highland Folk Festival, and Wheelwright's Coal Camp Days Festival are but three examples. In Weeksbury, the old elementary school now serves as a community center; in Wheelwright, the old "colored" pool hall now serves as the senior citizens center, and the old boardinghouse/clubhouse that served the African American community is being rehabilitated as a therapeutic foster care facility; and in Martin, the old train depot is now a business. Many of the old coal camp houses are still used as residences, a testimony to the quality of construction of those homes.

This history is not comprehensive; people, communities, and events for which there are no currently available photographs have been excluded. Among the exclusions, perhaps the most significant is the 1958 school bus crash that claimed the lives the bus driver and of 26 children from the coal camps, a tragedy that changed the lives of everyone in the county.

This, then, is the story of coal and of railroads and how they helped to create the wonderful little corner of Kentucky known as Floyd County.

One

BEFORE THE COAL BOOM

While coal has been mined commercially in the United States since the 1700s, and the resources in Central Appalachia have been documented for nearly that long, it took a long time for investors, capitalists, and mineral speculators to seriously consider trying to access these reserves. The lack of ready transportation into and out of the area, the availability of the mineral in other, more accessible regions of the country, and the lack of workers for mining all served to discourage potential investors. With the dawn of the industrial age came a tremendous demand for coal. The ever-expanding inter-continental railroad system demanded coal to fire the engines; a burgeoning demand for steel for machinery, infrastructure projects, and other uses required coal for the coking process used to make steel. With this increased demand, the Central Appalachian reserves of southern West Virginia, eastern Kentucky, and western Virginia were suddenly more attractive to investors.

Visions of potential profits made investment in expensive infrastructure necessary to make these reserves accessible worthwhile. In some instances, the very investors who owned the railroads became mineral owners in Central Appalachia. The broad form deed, where property owners could sell the rights to the minerals under their land without giving up the land itself, became commonplace. Farmers, hungry for real cash, sold the rights to minerals that may or may not have been under their land for pennies an acre in what was probably the best investment deal the speculators ever found. Among those whose money poured into the region were well-known names: Rockefeller, Morgan, Roosevelt, Mellon, Forbes, and many others.

Unlike other industries that can be built where it is convenient, coal has to be mined where it is in the ground. When it is located in remote areas without established cities or towns nearby, the coal companies had to build towns to house and provide for the miners. These remote areas were sparsely populated, making it necessary to bring in workers from outside.

Before the mining era, Floyd County was primarily agrarian; small subsistence farming was a way of life for many of the families living here. This June 25, 1913, photograph shows two family homes and a large cornfield at Wheelwright; mining operations began in Wheelwright just three years later. (Courtesy of ALC.)

Prior to the development of easily navigable roads and the widespread use of automobiles, horse-drawn buggies were commonplace in Floyd County. Hitching posts were more common in the early coal camps than were parking spaces for automobiles. In this 1930 photograph, Mr. and Mrs. Milferd Hall ride along in their horse-drawn buggy at McDowell. (Courtesy of ALC.)

Taken from the vicinity of the Boy Scout Cabin, this photograph shows an elevated view of several commercial buildings in Wheelwright. Included from the left are the coal tipple, bathhouse, and elementary school. It appears that the negative was printed backward for this photograph, since the buildings are in reverse order from the actual layout of the town. (Courtesy of ALC.)

To open a mine, the coal companies must gain access to the coal seams. In this region, access is typically through a portal, or opening, driven into the side of a mountain. This type of underground mining, called slope or drift mining, involves a lateral entry into the coal seam. Trees are removed to allow a road to be cut into the hillside; the hillside then has to be stabilized with pilings to prevent slippage. Trees and other foliage above the mine portal are generally undisturbed, while that below the portal is cleared. This November 1948 image shows the Price Mine Project near Wheelwright as the area is prepared for a new mine. (Courtesy of ALC.)

In this elevation view of early Wayland taken around 1914–1915, early commercial structures are already in place. On the left, the larger building is a hotel, and the smaller building is a train depot. To the right, from front to back, are the jail, office building, bank, an unidentified building, the Methodist church, and the school. At center is a turntable where locomotives could be manually turned. (Courtesy of WHS.)

This 1915 photograph of Wayland shows many more structures in the town. The hotel in the previous picture is shown here from the back at the center of the photograph. Note the row of miners' homes in the background. (Courtesy of WHS.)

Although much of the early investment in coal in Floyd County came from outside the region, some locals did benefit from the exposure. In this photograph, John C. C. Mayo (third from left) leads a group of geologists, capitalists, and other speculators on an exploratory trip through eastern Kentucky. Although this rest stop was photographed in neighboring Pike County, the expedition also came through Floyd County. (Courtesy of ALC.)

The primary means of transportation in the Big Sandy Valley and much of eastern Kentucky was the push boat. Used to transport goods to markets in the region and to ship produce to markets in Louisa and beyond, the Big Sandy River was important to commercial development in Floyd County. This group on an outing was photographed by the John C. C. Mayo expedition. (Courtesy of ALC.)

14

Two

RAIL DEVELOPMENT OPENS DOORS TO GROWTH

Much of Floyd County—indeed, most everything south of the current path of U.S. 23—was sparsely inhabited prior to the early 20th century. With few roads, no navigable rivers away from the northern end of the county, and no railroads, the inhabitants were isolated from much of the rest of the county. Many early investors in the mineral rights, however, also had influence with the railroad companies. When the demand for coal and the price it would bring made it impossible to ignore the wealth lying underground, these investors used every political and industrial contact available to bring about the construction of railroads into these isolated areas.

Early rail construction in the mountains was done by private companies; dozens of small spurs were built by these companies. The Long Fork Railway Company, for example, provided service from Martin to Weeksbury, serving coal camps along the Left Fork of Beaver Creek, including Martin, Hite, Salisbury, McDowell, Wheelwright, Weeksbury, and, later, Drift, Ligon, and other communities that sprang up along the line. These small, private companies were eventually merged under the ownership of major railway companies. In Floyd County, much of that early consolidation resulted in these small operations being absorbed into the Chesapeake and Ohio Railway (C&O) and the Baltimore and Ohio Railway (B&O). The B&O eventually sold its interests to the C&O, leaving it the sole provider of rail service in the county.

LONG FORK RAILWAY COMPANY

TIME TABLE NO. 1

Friday, March 1, 1918

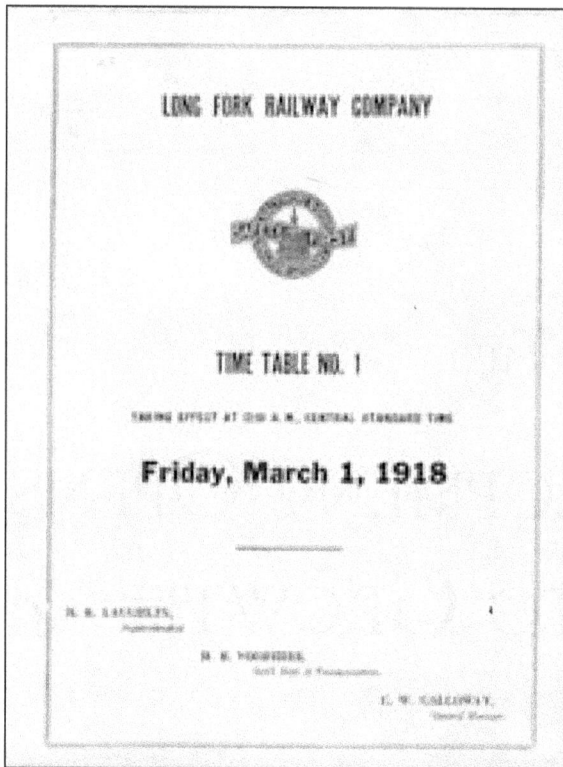

Train service to the coal camps along the Left Fork of Beaver Creek from Martin to Weeksbury was initiated with the Long Fork Railway Company. Service along this line commenced in March 1918. As indicated on the second photograph, the communities along the line in those early runs included Martin, Hite, Salisbury, Gibson, McDowell, Borders, Gearhart, Clear Creek, Buckingham, Wheelwright, and Weeksbury. Drift was only an on-demand passenger stop at this time. Note the limited availability of telephone service to the trains, with phones only available at the Martin and Weeksbury depots. As more coal camps were established, the tracks were extended, more stations were added, and rail service helped those communities to grow. (Both courtesy of COHS.)

WESTWARD   EASTWARD

SPECIAL RULES

The establishment of rail lines through the county was not sufficient to meet the needs of the individual coalmines. Side tracks had to be built to the coal tipples to connect them to the main rail lines. This undated photograph shows the side tracks of the Goodin and Barney Coal Company at Garrett. (Courtesy of ALC.)

A surveyor and rodman for the C&O lay out new tracks at Martin about 1920. In these early years of service, expansion of rail services was an ongoing process, and scenes such as these were commonplace. The photographer for this photograph was standing where the present depot is located, and a large engine terminal is now where the engines are standing. (Courtesy of COHS.)

This photograph of railroad tracks, depot, and siding on the C&O line near Weeksbury was taken about 1925. The twin columns of steam indicate the arrival of a train into town. (Courtesy of COHS.)

To protect trains and their passengers and cargo, the rails had to be regularly inspected. In this 1954 photograph, a trackwalker for the C&O's Big Sandy Subdivision rides a velocipede along the tracks for a close-up look at conditions. A velocipede is a track-riding vehicle that is pedaled like a bicycle. (Courtesy of COHS.)

After picking up coal at David, the Middle Creek Shifter with H-4 No. 144 slows at Permele to pull loads from Princess Elkhorn No. 2 mine in this June 1954 photograph. The mine is gone, but those camp houses, now privately owned, are still used. It is likely these houses were used by officials of Princess Coals. The head brakeman is ready to drop off the side of the engine. (Courtesy of COHS.)

Passenger train no. 36, behind E-8 No. 4009, glides through Cliff, Kentucky, just north of Prestonsburg in June 1954. In the siding (side track) is no. 97 with its characteristic perishable reefers. A wisp of steam in the front indicates that Big Sandy is not dieselized entirely. (Courtesy of COHS.)

The Beaver Creek morning train no. 280 is shown at Allen in the 1920s. Note the proximity of both homes and what appear to be commercial buildings along the tracks. Allen is also near the Big Sandy River, making it a good location for trade. The depot sits between the track and the siding, just to the left of the train. (Courtesy of COHS.)

Passengers prepare to board the train at the Martin station in this 1940s photograph. Riders from the southern sections of Floyd County would take the train to Martin, then switch to other trains on the Big Sandy Line for transportation to Louisa, Huntington, Lexington, or other towns outside the local mining area. (Courtesy of COHS.)

20

In this photograph, taken about 1954, a C&O 7084 diesel locomotive heads a pair of ABA F7s with a coal train northbound on the Big Sandy Subdivision near Prestonsburg. The Levisa Fork of the Big Sandy River flows on the left side of the train. (Courtesy of COHS.)

A C&O manifest freight and passenger local train is seen on the mainline near Marrowbone in the summer of 1958. (Courtesy of COHS.)

In late January 1957, Floyd County experienced the worst flooding since 1862, at the height of the Civil War. It remains one of the worst, if not the worst, natural disasters the area has experienced since that time. The Prestonsburg depot is shown in the upper photograph, floodwaters clearly threatening both the depot and tracks. Passengers, area residents, and others have gathered on the tracks to wait for their trains and to watch the floodwaters. Trash and debris fill both the river and areas where the water has receded and can be seen collecting along the track near the bottom of the picture. The lower photograph, taken by Everett Young two decades later, shows the Prestonsburg depot still in operation. (Courtesy of COHS.)

The Lackey depot on the C&O is a standard boxcar design commonly used throughout the region. In many places, actual boxcars were converted for use as depots. This early 1950s photograph shows automobiles, likely belonging to workers, and a distant house that may belong to a local miner or rail worker. (Courtesy of COHS.)

This photograph of the C&O depot at Harold was taken during the flood of 1957. A motorcar sits on the tracks; an unidentified passenger (far left) and four unidentified rail workers stand nearby. (Courtesy of COHS.)

This 1968 photograph by Everett Young shows the old yard office at Martin. The building was a modification of the standard boxcar architecture used by the C&O for depots on its lines. (Courtesy of COHS.)

A fully loaded coal train backs out of Wheelwright in this 1946 Russell Lee photograph. There was no place in town for trains to turn around, making it necessary for them to back out of town with their cargoes. Note the proximity of the miners' homes to the tracks. Coal dust was the most common household cleaning problem for miners whose homes lay along the railroad tracks. (Courtesy of NA.)

Conveyors carry coal from the mine to the coal tipple at Princess Elkhorn Coal at David around 1954. Loaded coal cars wait for delivery to their final destination. Coal tipples, also called preparation plants, sort and wash the coal before loading it waiting coal cars for train passage to distribution centers or customers. (Courtesy of COHS.)

This April 12, 1949, photograph by the Kentucky and West Virginia Power Company shows the complex series of facilities and conveyors required to prepare coal from the mine for shipment to Inland Steel Company's steel production facilities and external customers. Empty coal cars wait to be pulled through where they will be filled with coal for shipment. (Courtesy of COHS.)

This 1944 photograph of Inland Steel Company's coal tipple at Wheelwright, taken from the opposite direction from the previous photograph, shows coal being transferred from the facility into a waiting coal car. A covered conveyor, shown on the right through the trees, carries coal from the mine into the tipple for preparation and loading. (Courtesy of COHS.)

Inland Steel Company's huge Price preparation plant was the largest such facility on the C&O in 1953, loading over 3,000 fifty-ton railcars monthly. Cleaner coal was also brought in from other mines by rail to be processed through the plant. It operated until early 1991. (Courtesy of COHS.)

This April 12, 1949, photograph by the Kentucky and West Virginia Power Company of the Koppers Coal Company coal tipple at Weeksbury shows empty coal cars waiting to be filled with coal for shipment. The facilities in the different coal camps served the same purpose, to prepare coal for shipment, but the condition of the structures varied widely. (Courtesy of COHS.)

This April 12, 1949, photograph by the Kentucky and West Virginia Power Company shows the central preparation plant for Elkhorn Coal at Wayland. Coal companies began branding their coals in the early 20th century. This facility produced what the company advertised as "Flaming Horsepower Coals." (Courtesy of COHS.)

This undated photograph of the Central Preparation Plant of the Elkhorn Coal Company in Wayland shows five tracks coming through the preparation plant, each with loaded coal cars ready to ship out. (Courtesy of COHS.)

An unidentified switchman works to direct the trains onto their proper tracks in this undated photograph. His job is critical in protecting the trains and their cargo as they move along the rails through the Big Sandy Subdivision. (Courtesy of COHS.)

Train derailments were a danger faced by the coal companies and rail operators. At least four coal cars have derailed in this spring 1922 accident. The cars were above the tunnel and had to be snaked through from the Big Sandy side of the tunnel. Although the photograph identifies the location as Wayland, there were no train tunnels at Wayland. It is impossible to identify at which of the few tunnels in the area the derailment actually occurred. (Courtesy of COHS.)

Trains operate at the old engine house at Martin in this September 19, 1971, photograph. Freight cars line the tracks as the water tower stands watch over the scene. It is only fitting to leave the chapter on rail history with another piece of history, a caboose at the old engine house. For many years in the late 20th century, the caboose disappeared from trains; without them, the trains seemed incomplete. Like a sentence without a period, the train seemed to end badly, or not at all. A recent resurgence in the use of the caboose seems an acknowledgement from the rail companies that some history and nostalgia is worth reviving. (Courtesy of COHS.)

Three

COAL CAMP LIFE

Unlike other industries that can be built where it is convenient, coal has to be mined where it is in the ground. When it was located in remote areas without established cities or towns nearby, the coal companies had to build towns to house and provide for the miners. These remote areas were sparsely populated, making it necessary to bring in workers from outside.

Life in the coal camps was not a single, homogenous event experienced the same way by everyone who lived in them. From camp to camp, and even within the individual camps, experiences and quality of life depended on the perspective of the individual. Everything from economic conditions to living conditions, race relations to cultural experiences, and entertainment to schools was unevenly shared. The common thread connecting everyone living in these camps, however, was the coal company. The company was the boss, landlord, shop keeper, police, pastor, teacher, and parent. Because the company owned the mine and the town, and everything in the town, it had complete control over who came and left, who could live within its borders, and who could visit the residents and businesses. In other words, it could exact complete control over the lives of those who lived there. It paid wages to miners as well as to those who worked in the various businesses established in town, it hired the police officers, and frequently it built the churches and schools. The company acted as a father, making decisions about who could have home additions made or move to a larger home. It decided what types of entertainment venues to build, what types of goods to stock in the company stores, where miners and their families would live and work, and what types of amenities were needed.

In some camps, conditions were as modern as any American city; in others, conditions resembled the worst to be found in any third-world nation. The reality of miner mobility, however, reduced the likelihood of company abuse. The following images provide a sense of conditions in the communities of Floyd County.

On the banks of the Big Sandy River lies Prestonsburg, the county seat of Floyd County. In this 1880s photograph of the town, the agrarian feel of the county is still part of the county seat. The neatly laid-out streets lie along fields, all nestled within the mountains that surround the community. (Courtesy of ALC.)

The Conley family has roots deep in Knott, Magoffin, and Floyd Counties. John David Conley, shown in this 1852 photograph, is the progenitor of most of the Conleys throughout this region. (Courtesy of ALC.)

In this 1920 photograph taken on Front Street in Wayland, Marie Daniels is standing in the street while Hazel Daniels watches from the front porch of a house. (Courtesy of WHS.)

In this undated photograph of Main Street in Wheelwright, the buildings that would later make the town renowned for its architecture were not in place. Wood frame structures, rather than the later-famed brick ones, lined the streets. On the right side of the street, from front to back, are the post office, clubhouse/hotel, office building, and company store. (Courtesy of ALC.)

This 1973 photograph shows the community of Glo Hollow, which leads into the Glo coal camp. The Estill coal camp can be seen in the background. The photograph was taken from Glo Hill before the Turner houses were built. (Courtesy of ALC.)

In this elevated view of Wheelwright, the entire commercial district, as well as the residential areas known as 79 Hill and Apartment Hill, is visible. The wood-frame commercial structures set the date prior to the major World War II–era renovations that included bricking those buildings. (Courtesy of ALC.)

Coal camp housing had sameness about it; companies worked from a minimum of house plans and built houses as closely together as possible in order to accommodate the most employees. In general, the houses were either unpainted or painted white. Roofs may be shingle, slate, or tin. This 1920s photograph shows the houses along "Silk Stocking Row" in Wayland. (Courtesy of WHS.)

The Anderson children of Wayland play in the back alley from fire breaks down in this undated picture. They are, from left to right, Larry, Karen, Gayle, and Johnny. Like children in many coal camps, or in any small town, the children find ways to entertain themselves outside on nice days. (Courtesy of WHS.)

In Weeksbury, this line of wood-frame homes lies parallel to a polluted creek running through the camp. Children play beside the house in the foreground; rough wood-plank footbridges allow passage across the creek. (Courtesy of ALC.)

Adm. Joel T. Boone chats with a coal miner and his four children outside their unpainted home in Weeksbury in this June 8, 1946, photograph. The house is an unpainted wood-frame structure in desperate need of repairs. Boone was working with a group of government employees and military officers to document health conditions in the coal camps. (Courtesy of NA.)

A large load of laundry hangs outside to dry in Hall Hollow, a predominantly African American community in Wheelwright. In the early 20th century, it was not uncommon for wives of miners to take in laundry of single men and company executives. This photograph was taken on September 24, 1946, by Russell Lee. (Courtesy of NA.)

Many cars and trucks sit along an unpaved road in this undated photograph. Miners' houses line both sides of the street. (Courtesy of ALC.)

With the release of the Brownie, the first mass-produced camera, in 1900, and the rapid development of improved cameras, film, and flash technology, it became more affordable for families to purchase personal cameras. In the upper photograph, children play in the snow at Stampers Branch. Standing, from left to right, are Judy Stewart, Robert L. Stewart, Billy J. Vincent, Paul Robinson, and Richard Moore. In the photograph at left, McDowell resident Aggie Paige, seated, holds son Delman while other sons stand. The sons are, from left to right, Blaine, James, Truman, and McDowell. They are seated outside a wood-frame structure, perhaps their home, in 1942. (Above courtesy of Marionette Burgess, left courtesy of ALC.)

Russell Lee captured this photograph of the Fain family on September 27, 1946. Pictured are, from left to right, Harry Ray (age 15), Ella Jane (age 18), Harry (age 45), Hattie (age 43), Geraldine (age 22), and George (age 20) Harry was a coal loader at Inland Steel Company's mine in Wheelwright. (Courtesy of NA.)

Friends and family gather on the front porch of the Fain home in Wheelwright on a Sunday afternoon. Visiting among the families was perhaps the most common form of socialization that took place in the coal camps. This photograph was taken by Russell Lee on September 22, 1946. (Courtesy of NA.)

Wheelwright coal miner Henry Armour poses with his family in this September 26, 1946, photograph. One of the top coal loaders at the mine, his 1945 income was reported to be in excess of $5,400. In this photograph are, from left to right, Rozella, Essie Lee, Elizabeth (wife) holding grandson Henry L. (son of Rozella), Henry, Ernest, and Mattie Lee. (Courtesy of NA.)

Two board-and-batten homes are pictured in the Hall Hollow section of Wheelwright. Six young girls stand on the porch watching, while two men are washing and waxing a car next to the creek in this September 1946 photograph by Russell Lee. Other automobiles are visible in the distance. (Courtesy of NA.)

The Triplet children, Willie (left) and Virgil, pose for a photograph near a bridge over the creek at Bevinsville between the communities of Hi Hat and Wheelwright. Although undated, the picture was taken around 1924–1925. (Courtesy of ALC.)

In this undated photograph, Melvin residents Pearl Hall (left) and Della Hall stand on the steps while Caroly McEay (left) and Grady Tackett stand on the ground in front of a wood-frame house. Melvin camp sits just outside Weeksbury, between Weeksbury and Wheelwright. (Courtesy of ALC.)

Wheelwright coal miner Temis Sullivan's wife shows off her kitchen to Russell Lee during his visit to Wheelwright in this September 24, 1946, photograph. By 1946, all the homes in Wheelwright already had fully functional kitchens featuring electric appliances and gas-powered cooking stoves. It also had indoor bathroom facilities including flush toilets. They also used natural gas pumped from gas wells in the town for cooking and heating. Notice the modern appliances and decorative touches. Although not everyone had Sullivan's design flair, the kitchen itself is not unusual for the Wheelwright camp. (Courtesy of NA.)

"Bad" John Hall stands with his arm around a man wearing a coal miner's cap and boots. John Hall wears a suit with his badge on his vest and side arms nearly hidden beneath his jacket in this undated photograph. The location is not certain, but is likely in Wheelwright. (Courtesy of ALC.)

When "Bad" John Hall passed away in 1931, the community mourned. Here, over 100 people gather at the cemetery to mark John's passing. (Courtesy of ALC.)

On Main Street in Wheelwright, an unidentified African American man wearing a badge is captured in this September 1946 Russell Lee photograph. Many cars are parked along the street behind this man. Buildings in the photograph include (from front to back) the elementary school, a miner's house, the movie theater, and the community hall. (Courtesy of NA.)

The community hall in Wheelwright was a two-story structure with columns along the front. It included a post office, restaurant, barbershop, soda fountain, and drugstore downstairs and a dance hall upstairs. To the right of the community hall is the theater building. The company store, administration offices, and clubhouse sit across the street. (Courtesy of ALC.)

44

Four

COMMUNITY SERVICES

Community services in the coal camps were primarily based in the coal camps. Other than matters that had to be dealt with at the county courthouse, law enforcement, fire protection, health care, water and sanitary sewers, street construction and maintenance, barber and beauty shops, libraries, and shopping facilities were generally provided for in the coal camps. When the coal companies built towns, they had to create the infrastructure needed to fully sustain the community. The availability and quality of services varied from camp to camp, but the necessity to provide for the most essential needs was inextricably linked to the preservation of the coal company's investment in the community. They served to provide continued income through recovery of the payroll dollars expended, protection against intentional and unintentional property loss, and increased productivity of workers who did not have to travel to the county seat for essentials.

Because miners' families also lived in the camps, the company had a readily available pool of potential employees for these additional services. For these families, the creation of additional jobs also represented the potential for improved quality of life through access to additional services and through the increased family income that came from adding second or even third paychecks to the family coffers. In some families, this represented the difference between being in debt to the company store and being able to save money to buy an automobile or to invest in a piece of land or a home outside the camp.

Water and sanitary sewer systems also served the coal company and families through improved community health, representing both a reduction in demand for medical services and in workdays lost due to illness. Toward this end, some coal camps also engaged the services of nutritionists through county extension offices to help teach better practices in housekeeping and cooking. Better nutrition and improved sanitation helped to achieve better overall conditions for everyone in the camps.

Admiral Boone and Comdr. John H. Balch stand outside the clubhouse with mine managers. They are standing outside the entrance to the hotel lobby and restaurant; a lawn jockey stands on the sidewalk in front of them in this June 1946 Russell Lee photograph. (Courtesy of NA.)

The heart of the county seat is the county courthouse; this 1890 photograph of the new county courthouse in downtown Prestonsburg was a step into modernity. As coal began to take hold in the region, growth and investment at all levels of government and the community escalated. This new construction was part of that investment. (Courtesy of ALC.)

In many coal camps, the coal company constructed small hospitals to deal with emergencies among miners and miners' families. In this photograph, three doctors and three nurses (doctors are male, nurses female) pose outside the Wheelwright Hospital. Later, the United Mine Workers of America established the Miners Hospitals throughout Appalachia, including the Floyd County location at McDowell. (Courtesy of NA.)

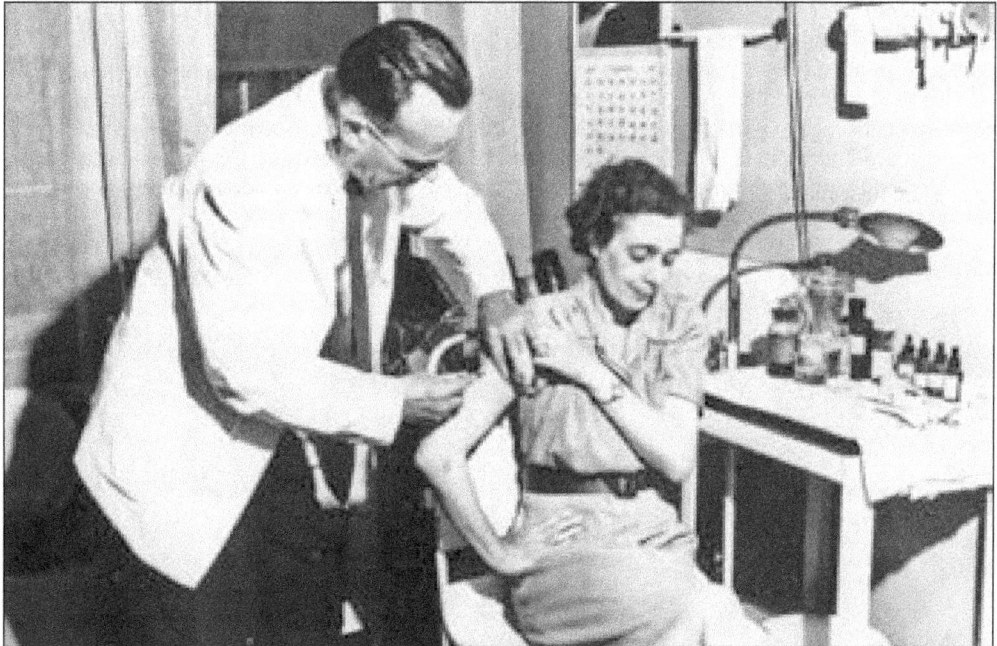

Dr. Bailey administers an injection to the wife of a miner at Inland Steel Company's company hospital in Wheelwright. The hospital provided services to families of coal miners as well as for miners who were injured inside the mine. The hospital provided basic laboratory services, X-rays, and minor surgeries in addition to general medical care. This photograph was taken on September 24, 1946, by Russell Lee. (Courtesy of NA.)

In addition to meeting the shopping needs of the coal camps, company stores provided a place for residents to congregate and exchange news from the community. Miners, or members of their families, could go into these stores and buy needed items on credit or lease and have the payments deducted from their paychecks. Usually, the company set a dollar amount that could be charged based on the miner's anticipated weekly wages. Services and goods varied from coal camp to coal camp in these stores, but they all provided essential groceries and household items. In the upper photograph, Ray Long (left) and Pat Murray work inside the meat market at the Wayland company store in the 1920s. Below, a large crowd of miners and mine families shops in the company store in Wayland. (Both courtesy of WHS.)

The building in this photograph was an early company store in Wheelwright. It was later modernized by Inland Steel Company. Several years later, the building burned and was replaced by a new company store. The company store was added to the National Register of Historical Places in 1980 and today serves as a home for Lighthouse Temple Church. (Courtesy of ALC.)

Two unidentified workers tend the men's apparel section in the clothing store in Wheelwright. Inland Steel Company operated stores selling everything from apparel to furniture to groceries; workers could purchase their goods on lease, a form of credit extended by the coal company to employees. This photograph was taken on September 26, 1946, by Russell Lee. (Courtesy of NA.)

This photograph shows the only major parking lot in Wheelwright. Taken on December 13, 1953, it shows parking for the bathhouse (which is just off camera to the left), the cleaning plant, two miners' houses, and, on the hill, the Boy Scout cabin. (Courtesy of ALC.)

The community building in Wheelwright was a hub of social activity. The upper floor contained a dance hall that hosted dances with live music on the weekends and provided space for high school dances and other community gatherings. The lower floor included a barbershop, post office, and soda fountain. This photograph was taken September 21, 1946, by Russell Lee. (Courtesy of NA.)

During the Great Depression, times were tough for everyone. Residents of the coal camps were no exception. In this 1932 photograph, relief clients in Wheelwright (those who received governmental assistance) wait in line. In the background, the school building, bathhouse, and coal tipple are visible. (Courtesy of ALC.)

In this undated early photograph of Wheelwright, many of the first commercial structures are already in place. Situated near the railroad tracks are, from left to right, the clubhouse, which housed several businesses and lodging for single white miners; the company store; and the train depot. Opposite these buildings are, from left to right, the community center and the theater. Houses and apartments are terraced on the hillside. (Courtesy of ALC.)

Two unidentified men stand on the small front porch at the Inland Steel Company gas station in Wheelwright. In the front are two sets of gas pumps selling leaded gasoline. The gas station was the only one in town. This Russell Lee photograph was taken on September 21, 1946. (Courtesy of NA.)

This view of Main Street in Wheelwright shows many of the commercial buildings in town. On the left side of the road are the train depot, "colored" fountain, repair shop, gas station (only pumps are visible), and the company store. A small, freestanding traffic light is visible between the fountain and depot. This photograph was taken by Russell Lee on September 24, 1946. (Courtesy of NA.)

In coal camps, the coal company was responsible for all aspects of life; this fire truck was necessary to protect the company's investment in commercial and residential structures in the town at a time when county fire protection was impractical for these remote communities. The truck sits at Wheelwright City Hall; the building housed a police court, fire department, city offices, and city jail. (Courtesy of ALC.)

For residents of the coal camps without access to an automobile, Prestonsburg-based Sparks Brothers Bus Company provided service between the coal camps and the county seat. John P. Wells (left) and Junior Wells (right) are shown with an unidentified man with bus no. 103 in the late 1940s. (Courtesy of WHS.)

Members of the Wheelwright town board and police department gather in front of the new municipal building. This new facility included a jail in the basement as well as housing the police department, police court, and fire department. Included are, from left to right, Earl Blackburn, Bob Moscrip, Gus Little, C. R. "Bob" Miller, Kenneth "K. B." Deal, Bill Rose, H. M. Wilkinson, Doctor Bailey, and Charlie Hanger. This photograph was taken September 26, 1946, by Russell Lee. (Courtesy of NA.)

Five

Work Life

The very existence of the coal camp was predicated on one purpose: the extraction of coal. Whether the camp was owned by a steel producer who wanted coal for its own use or by a coal company with markets in the United States and abroad to supply, the goal was the same. They needed to extract as much coal as possible and practical at the lowest possible cost.

For coal miners, the work was the same from camp to camp and from mine to mine; the means of accomplishing that work, the conditions in which the work was done, and the safety with which the work could be accomplished were not always the same. Miners were responsible for extracting the coal from deep inside the mountain, for installing curtains for ventilation, for putting in timbers to secure the roof, and for laying the tracks needed to haul the coal out after it was removed from the seam.

In some mines, the coal seam was barely 3 feet thick; in others, it may be as high as 10 feet. In the lower coal seams, miners accomplished their work on their knees, working for hour after hour in 60-degree temperatures loading tons of coal and securing their workspace. Sometimes the mines were wet, making working conditions even worse because of the layer of mud the miners had to walk or crawl through. The presence of methane gas, a highly toxic and explosive gas that forms during the same process that creates coal, was also a daily reality. Mine ventilation systems helped to dilute the gas, but accidents or inadequate ventilation could lead to disaster.

Other differences in mine operations came from the level of mechanization in the mine. As machines came into use, the work became easier for the miners, but available jobs decreased. Mechanized mines could produce more coal with fewer workers. Mechanization started slowly at the beginning of the 20th century but was not fully integrated into most mine operations until the 1950s.

Miners in this new mine have new equipment to use. Outside the portal on the right sits a loader. Often called a Joy Loader for the company most noted for production of the equipment, it is used to scoop up coal and load it into waiting coal cars or conveyors to be hauled out of the mine. (Courtesy of ALC.)

Opening a new mine in these early days took a lot of hard work. Miners in this photograph are using basic tools including shovels and wheelbarrows to remove material from the new portals; timbers lying about will be used to support the roof to prevent falls. (Courtesy of WHS.)

Employees of Elkhorn Coal Company at Wheelwright sit outside a maintenance building in 1923. Although their jobs are not identified, the saw and hammer shown would indicate they were likely part of the construction crew, responsible for everything from building to maintenance of commercial and residential structures. Elkhorn owned and operated the mine and town until selling out to Inland Steel Company in 1930. (Courtesy of ALC.)

In the early days of mining, animal-drawn carts like the one shown here were used to haul coal out of the mines. Horses and mules were the most common animals used for this purpose. Here Jim Vanderpool rides his coal cart out of the mine near Garrett, Kentucky. (Courtesy of ALC.)

Four unidentified men pose with a wooden coal cart in this early-20th-century photograph. The hats, dress shirts, and ties would seem to indicate the men are not miners; they definitely have not just come up from a mine. A new building is under construction in the background. (Courtesy of WHS.)

In this September 1, 1949, photograph, a view up the west side of the Price Mine Project near Wheelwright shows the conveyor gallery toward the west screen house and head house. Early-model cars can be seen in the foreground. (Courtesy of ALC.)

One hundred coal miners have gathered at the Hi Hat camp near the Elkhorn Clear Creek Mines in this undated photograph. Elkhorn Coal Company was a major coal operator throughout Floyd County and was responsible for the initial construction of many of the coal camps. (Courtesy of ALC.)

In this slightly elevated view, several empty coal cars can be seen going into the tipple at Wheelwright. The wooden tipple, which stood at the site of the old Lee Hall home place, was later replaced by an all-steel-and-concrete structure, the first of its kind in eastern Kentucky. (Courtesy of NA.)

A coal tipple, cleaning plans, and aerial tram are seen in this 1933 photograph taken in Wheelwright. Many coal cars, both loaded and unloaded, sit on the tracks. (Courtesy of ALC.)

Seven coal miners, wearing mining hard hats and carrying lunch pails, walk out of the mine owned by Inland Steel Company at Wheelwright. Another miner is partially visible in the foreground. This photograph was taken by Russell Lee in September 1946. (Courtesy of NA.)

Comdr. John H. Balch (left, back to camera), Adm. Joel T. Boone (center, facing camera), and Edwin R. "Jack" Price (far right) meet with several unidentified coal miners at Wheelwright. Boone was commissioned to conduct an investigation into conditions in the bituminous coal industry; the Russell Lee photographs used throughout this book were part of his report. This photograph was taken September 23, 1946, by Lee. (Courtesy of NA.)

Harry Fain was a coal loader for the Inland Steel Company's mine at Wheelwright. The coal loaders' job involved working alone to extract the coal from the seam, load it for removal from the mine, and secure the workplace so he could continue to work safely. Photographs on the next several pages will show Harry as he goes about his work on a typical workday. Note the hard hat he wears on his head; it holds a battery-powered mining lamp that will provide his only illumination while he works underground. Under his right arm is a lunch bucket. Miners' meals come when they are hungry, not at any specific time. They work until they need sustenance, and break for a meal in the mine. Running water for washing up is not available, and lunch can be a solitary meal unless others working in other nearby rooms (work areas) are ready for a break at the same time. (Courtesy of NA.)

One of the early steps in mining coal involved cutting along the bottom of the coal seam either with a pick or a cutting machine. This undercutting allows for the coal to be blasted more efficiently without excessive fracturing. Undercutting machines were commercially available but not in use at the Wheelwright mine. This September 24, 1946, Russell Lee photograph shows Wheelwright miner Harry Fain using a pick to undercut the seam where he is working. (Courtesy of NA.)

One of the dangers facing miners is the potential for roof falls. Here Harry is placing and securing timbers (wood posts) and checking for loose rocks that could potentially fall and cause injury. Because he is responsible for securing his own work area, this work is critical for ensuring his own safety. (Courtesy of NA.)

In the upper photograph, Harry Fain assembles an auger he will use for drilling holes to load explosive charges in the face of the mine. As shown in the lower photograph, the auger is used in conjunction with a breast plate that will allow the miner to put his weight behind the auger while drilling. This allows him to drill holes into the coal more easily. Machines had been invented to complete this task but were not in use at the Wheelwright mine yet. These photographs were taken September 24, 1946, by Russell Lee. (Both courtesy of NA.)

After drilling holes in the face of the mine with his auger, Harry will load the holes with blasting powder in preparation for detonating it to break coal loose from the seam. (Courtesy of NA.)

Stooping low in the mine, Harry Fain shovels coal into waiting coal cars. On a typical workday, he will shovel between 16 and 17 tons of coal into waiting coal cars before heading home. The height of a mine tunnel can vary widely, ranging from under 36 inches to over 10 feet. This photograph was taken September 24, 1946, by Russell Lee. (Courtesy of NA.)

In the upper photograph, Harry loads coal into a waiting coal car using a wide-blade shovel. Note the low height of the ceiling in the mine. In the lower photograph, he kneels in loose coal with the tools of his trade: a wide-blade shovel for loading, a pick for undercutting the coal, and a battery-powered lamp to light the dark tunnel. The rechargeable battery or his lamp is clipped to his belt at the back of his pants. He must clear this coal in order to extend tracks into this area. (Both courtesy of NA.)

As coal is removed from the mine, the tracks for the coal cars must be extended further underground. Before mechanization led to specialization underground, the coal loader was responsible for this task along with the actual mining operations. Here Harry Fain lays track at Inland Steel Company's Wheelwright mine. This photograph was taken September 24, 1946, by Russell Lee. (Courtesy of NA.)

Harry Fain discusses the day's work at the end of his morning shift at the Wheelwright Nos. 1 and 2 mines in this September 23, 1946, Russell Lee photograph. Typical topics for discussion might include roof conditions, progress in the room where he is working, or the amount of coal loaded for the day. (Courtesy of NA.)

Harry Fain undresses in a locker room in the Wheelwright bathhouse. These facilities were provided by many coal companies to allow miners to wash off the coal dust, mud, oil, and grime they were coated with at the end of the work shift. This photograph was taken September 23, 1946, by Russell Lee. (Courtesy of NA.)

This *c.* 1920 photograph shows a variety of commercial and residential structures around the Dinwood Railway Station near Martin. The rail station is the small structure at front, A. D. Osborne Dry Goods is behind the station, the crosstie yard is in the foreground, and the Alphoretta Post Office is to the right. (Courtesy of ALC.)

Twelve unidentified men pose at the Buck's Branch coal tipple in this 1934 photograph. Cars loaded with coal on the right will be emptied at the tipple for sorting and cleaning before being shipped off to market. (Courtesy of ALC.)

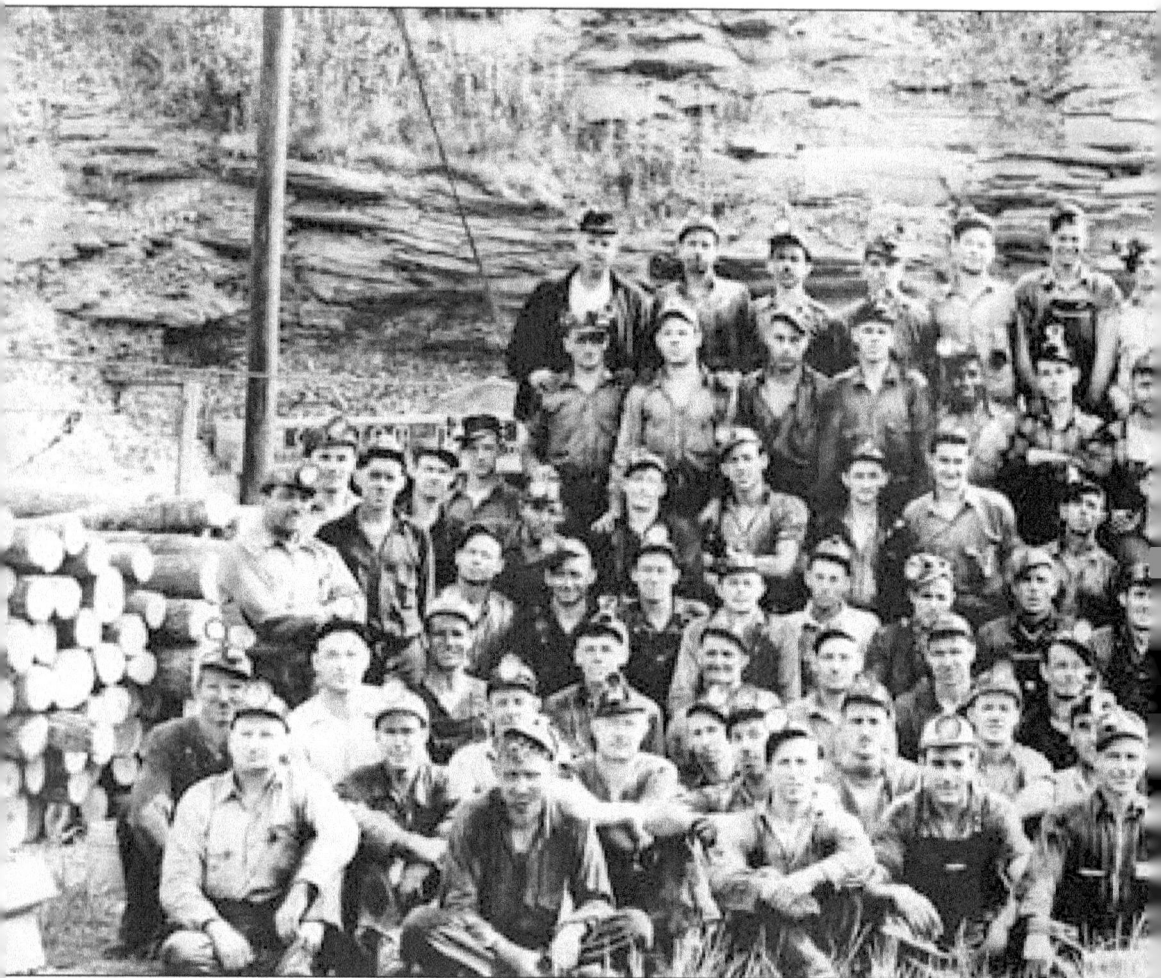

Mechanization was slow to be adopted in the mines of Floyd County. Elkhorn Coal Company's Blue Goose mine at Wayland is believed to be the first mechanized mine in Eastern Kentucky. The crew of that mine, shown on August 8, 1939, was the first in the area to be afforded the opportunity to learn to use the new equipment designed to make coal extraction easier, safer, and

more economical for the companies. Mechanization in the coal industry also led to a reduced need for miners, leading to a loss of jobs in the industry and in the region. Increased mechanization has cut the nation's mining workforce approximately 90 percent in the past 80 years. (Courtesy of WHS.)

The United Mine Workers of America (UMWA) had a bloody battle on their hands when they attempted to organize miners in eastern Kentucky and southern West Virginia. By the end of World War II, however, unions were common throughout the coalfields. This local UMWA meeting was held at one of the schools in Wheelwright on September 22, 1946; it was photographed by Russell Lee. Note that the union membership included both black and white miners. When founded in 1890, the UMWA was organized as an interracial union. Over its nearly 120-year history, there have been periods when the union did not always live up to that interracial ideal, but it remained an integral part of the union philosophy. (Both courtesy of NA.)

In photograph at right, a member of the mine rescue team at Wheelwright demonstrates how to use a breathing apparatus. A chart that shows how to assemble the breathing apparatus hangs on the wall behind him. Below, members of the mine rescue team try on equipment. Safety training was (and is) a critical component of training for coal miners. Methane gas occurs naturally in the seams of coal; this gas is highly toxic and explosive, creating two serious risks for underground miners. Ventilation in mines dilutes the methane to make it safe for workers, but in the event of an accident, this equipment is critical. The breathing apparatus allows rescue workers to enter methane-laden areas of the mine safely to rescue trapped or injured miners. These photographs were taken by Russell Lee on September 23, 1946. (Both courtesy of NA.)

Miners post inside the mine tunnel at Wheelwright on December 24, 1948. Operations at this mine were so extensive that there were portals, or openings, into the mine at both Buckingham and Price. Miners lay several hundred miles of track inside these tunnels. The tunnels were also used to transport food from the company store to miners in these other communities. (Courtesy of ALC.)

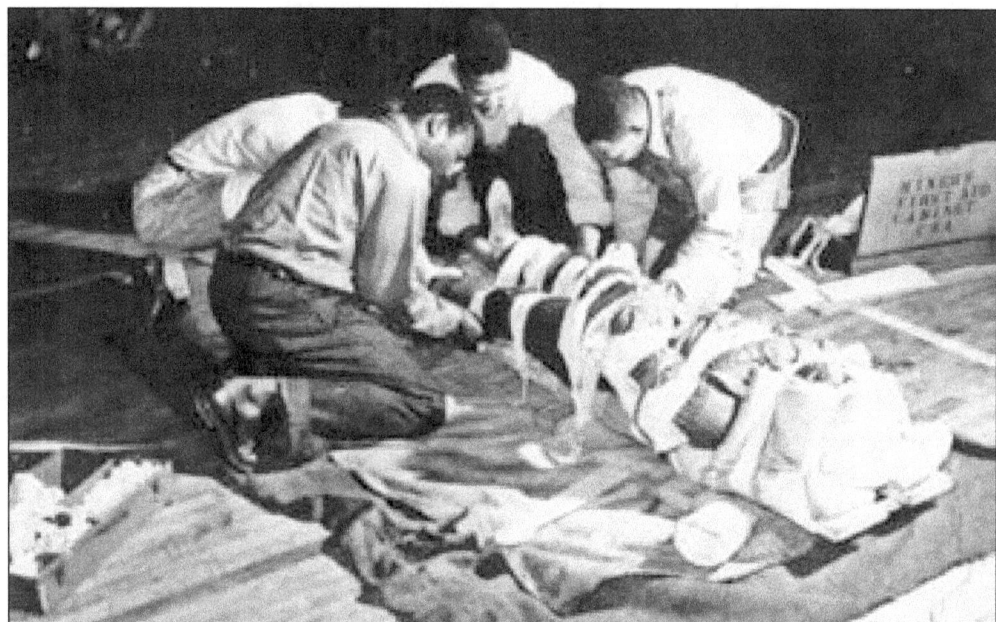

Five Wheelwright men, the 1945 state champion first aid team, practice first aid. Four work on wrapping and bandaging a fifth man who is lying on the boards. While the team events brought recognition, the real work came in their preparedness to deal with mine accidents. The skill they brought to the job could mean the difference between life and death for miners. (Courtesy of NA.)

Six

COAL CAMP BASEBALL

Many of the coal companies sponsored company baseball teams until into the late 1950s and early 1960s. These teams were often semi-professional and just as skilled and competitive as the professional baseball leagues. For the companies who engaged in the sport, baseball players were recruited for their skill on the diamond as much, or even more, than their experience in the mines. Company players were still miners, but in many instances, they were given less demanding jobs in the preparation plants or on the grounds of the camp instead of underground in the mine.

For professional and aspiring professional players, the coal camp teams represented a major stepping stone. They received a paycheck for working in the mines and, often, separate pay for playing ball. The players received recognition and, for the most skilled, the possibility of moving into the major leagues. For ball players with families, the possibility of playing on these teams provided a better and more stable income than coming up through the minor league teams in professional baseball. The recognition given to these semi-professional teams extended into the majors, and some players developed careers in professional baseball from these coal towns.

In the early 20th century, when professional baseball was still segregated and the players in the Negro Leagues were paid less than their white counterparts, coal camp baseball was also a good opportunity for African American players to earn good pay. Some players, like Richard Watts, moved from the Negro Leagues into coal camp baseball because the money was better. Watts played for the Birmingham Black Barons with Willie Mays prior to moving to the coalfields and playing for the Wheelwright baseball team.

Teams travelled extensively for games, with players from Floyd County playing against teams in West Virginia and western Virginia at times. Sunday afternoons in the coal camp was a time for baseball; large crowds would gather to cheer on their home teams. Fierce rivalries sprang up between the camps as they came out to support their players. For these coal camp heroes, baseball was much more than just a game.

Baseball commissioner, former U.S. senator, and former Kentucky governor A. B. "Happy" Chandler prepares to throw out the first pitch at the newly dedicated ballpark in Wayland in this 1948 photograph. Team members present for the event include, from left to right, J. C. "Crit" Wells, Mabry Martin, Ralph Thomas, Ray Patton, Ed Decoursey, Denver Collier, Thomas Boyd, Earl Branham, Parker Hobbs, Bill Frady, Willard Ratliff, Bob Hicks, an unidentified player behind Hicks, and another unidentified player off the right side. Chandler served as Kentucky's governor from 1935 until his resignation on October 9, 1939. He then served in the U.S. Senate until he resigned in 1945 to become Baseball commissioner, a post he held until his resignation on July 15, 1951. (Courtesy of WHS.)

The Lions Club dedication meeting in Wayland in September 1939 included many visiting dignitaries. Among those in attendance were, from left to right, (seated) Congressman Carl D. Perkins, Pikeville banker John M. Yost, Kentucky governor A. B. "Happy" Chandler, Lions Club district governor Fred Bullard, a state official of the Lions Club, Frank E. Harmon of Wayland, and Elkhorn Coal executive Col. Thomas S. Haymond; (standing) Delbert Webb, Quentin Terry, Edward Gibson, J. T. Spillman, Everett Williams, Ray Fraley, "Nat" Cooley, Ralph Wright, John "Zig" May, S. C. Berkeley, coach John Campbell, Jack Faull, Floyd Copley, Lawrence Price, Willard Castle, Jack Lyon, J. C. "Crit" Wells, unidentified, Russell Hundley, Johnny Wallace, unidentified, Dr. M. V. Wicker, unidentified, John Ratliff, and George E. Evans. (Courtesy of WHS.)

The 1940 Wayland Wasps pose near the ball field. They are, from left to right, (first row) Jack Branham, Mabry Martin, Willard Ratliff, Denver Collier, Bill Frady, Tommy Boyd, and Glen Nelson; (second row) Nick Martin, Blaine Martin, Parker Hobbs, and Earl Branham. (Courtesy of WHS.)

The Wayland baseball team poses in the late 1940s. The team includes, from left to right, (first row) Tommy Boyd, Mabry Martin, Bill Frady, Willard Ratliff, Dennis Crager, and Denver Collier; (second row) Ellis Layne, Parker Hobbs, Alton "Jack" Moore, and Danny Butcher; (third row) Carl Fraley, Charlie Adkins, Ed DeCoursey, Bob Hicks (manager), Earl Branham, and Bruce Lyons. (Courtesy of WHS.)

The Wheelwright baseball team was sponsored by Inland Steel Company in 1960. Players for the coal company teams travelled throughout the region, even into neighboring states, to play against other teams. Not long after this photograph was taken, coal company baseball teams passed into history. (Courtesy of Mary Lamm.)

Members of a David coal company baseball team pose for this c. 1941–1942 photograph. They include, from left to right, (first row) Billie Thompson, Sonny Carver, Glen Dixon, and Mr. Honeycutt; (second row) Joe Spears, Curtis Burchett, Billy Ratliff, Pete Everly, and Junion Durahan. (Courtesy of ALC.)

Wayland baseball player Ray Long poses with this vintage automobile on Front Street in the 1920s. Three children sit in a porch swing at the house behind him. (Courtesy of WHS.)

The Wheelwright coal mining baseball team for the 1948 playing season gathers outside for a team photograph. The team is dressed in their uniforms, and some of them are wearing their gloves. A board fence forms the background for the photograph. (Courtesy of ALC.)

Six

COAL CAMP SCHOOLS

Although the schools in any given county are officially under the control of the county school board, the coal companies frequently funded the construction of schools for children in the coal camps. The ownership and operation of these facilities varied from camp to camp. In some instances, the coal companies owned the facilities outright and leased the space to the school board. In others, the companies donated or sold the buildings to the school board. In any event, when the school was located on company property or when the company built or helped to build the schools on property outside the camp, it gained leverage within the school board. While hiring and firing decisions were the prerogative of the board of education, the coal companies were able to influence those decisions, to recommend people for hiring and firing, and to exert some level of pressure to help achieve their own goals for the schools.

Coal companies at times also sponsored sports or student groups that were based in the school. Safety teams for both boys and girls were popular; these teams competed regionally against teams from other coal camp schools. Such preparation helped to train these students for future work in the coal camp as well.

Typically the coal camp schools had most of the amenities of other public schools of the day. Science classes may or may not have had laboratory space, depending on need and space; music programs included school bands at some schools; basic courses in state-mandated curricula were available at all schools. A few of the schools also offered courses in Latin or in foreign languages. School cafeterias were not available in the early coal camp schools, but these were made available in later decades; when no cafeteria was available, students could bring lunches from home, go home for lunch, or in some camps, eat at the local restaurant or visit the local soda fountain.

The front and left side of the Wheelwright schoolhouse is shown in th undated photograph above. This frame structure, built before 1933, had wide steps leading to the school entrance and bell tower. In 1933, a school construction project necessitated moving the school and raising it to allow for the construction of a new lower floor. The lower photograph shows the school with the steps removed and pilings under the building to support it as it is jacked up for the addition. The front corner of the company bathhouse can be seen at the right and other company buildings at left. (Courtesy of ALC.)

In this 1933 photograph, the newly elevated school with its new basement is under construction; a second building has also been added to the facility. In 1980, this building was added to the National Register of Historical Places as part of Wheelwright's commercial district. The main building now serves as a private residence. (Courtesy of ALC.)

In late 1933, the new elementary school in Wheelwright was completed. The newly added facility would help the company accommodate the burgeoning number of children to be educated in town. This facility only served the children of white employees. School integration began one grade at a time shortly after the Supreme Court decision in *Brown vs. Board of Education*. (Courtesy of ALC.)

Ruth Rainey began her more-than-five-decade teaching career in the 1930s. When she began teaching, on Sundays she rode a mantrip (electric cart used to carry workers into and out of the mines) through the mine to the other side of the mountain, where she would spend the week with the family of one of her students, then ride back through the mountain again on Friday evening to spend the weekend at home with her family. One of 13 children, Rainey never married, but her extended family also includes the hundreds of children who passed through her classes in southern Floyd County. In these undated photographs, she is shown with her first-grade class at Wheelwright Elementary School. (Both courtesy of ALC.)

In this September 26, 1946, photograph by Russell Lee, children play during recess at Palmer Dunbar School in Wheelwright. Prior to construction of this school, African American children in the camp attended classes at Friendship Baptist Church. Under the direction of Principal Gilbert and teachers Sarah McQueen, Gladys Minor, Ms. Kaywod, Ms. Bishop, Gladys LaShore, and Mrs. Wilson, these children received education through high school. Integration in Wheelwright was staggered over a period of years; during that brief time, some of the white children in Wheelwright also attended this school. After the integration of the schools just over a decade later, the teachers and principal of the school left Wheelwright schools. (Courtesy of NA.)

School construction projects were common in the early decades of the coal camps. As the camps grew larger, it was only expected that facilities must expand to meet the needs of growing families. On the left is the Wayland High School building, constructed in 1941. To the right, behind the trees, is the old high school, constructed in 1928. (Courtesy of WHS.)

This late-1950s photograph shows Wayland's carnival court royalty. From left to right are (first row) Bud Martin, Wanda Slone, Jerry Fultz, Janie Muncy, Mike Cooley, Janet Harmon, Terry Samons, and Nancy Roope; (second row) Phillip Coleman, Mary B. Fraley, Connie Morrison, Rusty Fraley (on desk), unidentified, Claude Wes Frady, Debbie Hughes, Sara Fraley, unidentified, Linda Webb, and Phyllis Owsley; (third row) Bill Hall and Brenda Banks. (Courtesy of WHS.)

As the camps and schools matured, schools added bands. The Wayland High School Band included, from left to right, (first row) Becky Hall, Sharon Hayes, ? Vinson, Judy Price, and Flo Howard; (second row) Mary K. Smith, Jack Wicker, Kitty Branham, Zena Turner, Sue Slone, Jan Martin, and Judy Fraley; (third row) Glenna Little, unidentified, Maude Hatcher, Charlene Sexton, unidentified, Brenda Banks, Sandy Fraley, unidentified, and Mr. Price; (fourth row) Mary K. Slone, R. Cook, two unidentified, Hugh ?, Billie Frady, Donna Watkins, and C. Morgan. By the time this photograph was taken, likely in the early 1960s, there were well-established music programs at schools throughout the county. (Courtesy of WHS.)

Boys' high school athletics, particularly basketball and football, were mainstays of the coal camp schools. Girls were prohibited by state law from participating in competitive sports at this time; their activities were limited to cheerleading for the boys teams. In this photograph, the Wayland Wasps host a game against an unidentified team. (Courtesy of WHS.)

Until the 1950s, basketball was the preferred high school sport. In the upper photograph, players from Wayland High School's Wasps pose for the photographer. At right, on September 23, 1946, George Fain shoots a crip shot on the Wheelwright basketball court. As a 20-year-old World War II veteran, Fain is older than most of the other basketball players on the high school teams. (Above courtesy of WHS; right courtesy of NA.)

A group of about 30 students sits at their desks in class at Wheelwright High School in Wheelwright Junction. Although most of the students are children of miners at the Wheelwright mine, some live in surrounding areas and have no affiliation with the mine or Inland Steel. This photograph was taken September 25, 1946, by Russell Lee. (Courtesy of NA.)

Eighteen students are in a classroom at Wheelwright High School. George Fain, son of miner Harry Fain and a veteran of World War II, is a senior at the school. He is seated in the center, wearing a leather jacket. This photograph was taken by Russell Lee on September 23, 1946. (Courtesy of NA.)

Over 200 students gather for a school assembly in the auditorium at Wheelwright High School. Note that the boys and girls are seated separately for the event. Such separation was commonplace in official gatherings, although they did not maintain this separation in social or informal settings or in the classroom. This photograph was taken by Russell Lee on September 27, 1946. (Courtesy of NA.)

Soda fountains in coal camps were favorite hangouts for young people. The fountains provided a place where they could congregate, enjoy a snack or a soda, and hang out with their friends. This soda fountain was located on the street level of the Wheelwright community building. (Courtesy of NA.)

Wheelwright High School's graduating class of 1934 consisted of these 10 unidentified students. Here they stand outside the stone high school wearing their caps and gowns. (Courtesy of ALC.)

Eight

COAL CAMP CHURCHES

The sparsely populated areas that soon became home to coal camps were generally Protestant and, within the confines of Protestantism, were mostly Pentecostal and Baptist. When the coal companies began recruiting miners from other regions in the United States as well as from among Eastern European immigrants, there was an influx of Methodists, Episcopalians, Catholics, Jews, and many other religious backgrounds. The ability of a single coal camp to meet the spiritual needs of such diverse communities was seriously challenged. The need of the town to provide worship facilities for everyone was met by limitations of space within company-owned properties and the willingness of the coal company to finance construction of these facilities. For that reason, many houses of worship were shared by different denominations. They alternated days or weeks and scheduled services at different times of day; what evolved was a multi-purpose community worship center where there may be a Catholic service on odd-numbered Sunday mornings at 9, a Baptist service on even-numbered Sunday mornings at 11:00, a Pentecostal service on odd-numbered Sundays at noon, and so on. It became quite common for people to cross between the different Christian religions and attend services at several of the denominational services.

As the congregations became larger and more financially secure, some bought property outside the coal camp and constructed a church of their own. Scattered throughout rural Floyd County, it is possible to find dozens of small churches along the roadsides, between the towns, and on the hillsides just outside the coal camps. Some of these churches still see weekly use; others sit abandoned, as their congregations have moved away or died off in the decades since they were built.

The churches served as social centers, where youth groups, women's auxiliaries, prayer groups, and Bible study groups flourished. In some instances, they also served as schools until school buildings could be constructed. They served as a testament to the resilience and dedication of the faithful of the communities and to a willingness to exercise religious tolerance to accommodate the needs of the many.

Reverend Jones was the pastor of the church when this photograph was taken by Russell Lee on September 26, 1946. (Courtesy of NA.)

In the early days of Wheelwright, Friendship Baptist Church was shared by congregations of both races; it also was the school for African American students prior to construction of Palmer Dunbar School. Community groups also used the building for meetings.

The Methodist Church choir, photographed on September 23, 1946, by Russell Lee, was noted for its tremendous talent. The choir included Gonzell McClure (at piano) and Reverend Jackson (at pulpit on right) with, from left to right, (first row) Mrs. Rose, Mrs. Gilbert, Mrs. Coleman, Lola Melton, Ruth Helen Johnson, and Lilly Mae Thomas; (second row) unidentified, Gwynne Branham, and three unidentified; (third row) four unidentified and Mr. Coleman. (Courtesy NA.)

Baptismal pools in the churches were not generally found in the coal camps. When congregations met to baptize the newly converted, they gathered at the streams or creeks that were deep enough or at the closest river if there were not adequate streams or creeks nearby. Here, a local congregation

meets at Gobbler's Knob at Glo, a coal camp near Weeksbury and Estill operated by the Glo Gora Coal Company. (Courtesy of WHS.)

In the upper photograph, over 50 people, mostly miners from the Wheelwright community, gather in the small Baptist church tucked into a hillside at Wheelwright Junction. Below, the pastor at the church stands behind the pulpit addressing the congregation. Three unidentified men stand behind him. The church continued to serve the community for nearly 60 years after this September 22, 1946, photograph was taken; the congregation then built a new, larger facility at Wheelwright Junction. (Both courtesy of NA.)

When the coal company built this community church in Wheelwright, there was a cemetery already on the most suitable piece of land in town. That did not stop construction, however. The church (now a Methodist church) was built elevated above the graves with access to them through a side door. This church is still in use and is on the National Register of Historical Places. (Both courtesy of ALC.)

Seven young girls, about 12 years old, sit on a bench while their Sunday school teacher shares a Bible lesson at the Methodist church in Wheelwright. This photograph was taken by Russell Lee on September 22, 1946. (Courtesy of NA.)

Churchgoers gather at the dam behind the baseball park in Wayland for this 1920s baptism. Congregants gather on the hillside leading down to the water and sit in their cars to watch as the new members of their congregation, and perhaps their family members, are welcomed into the church. (Courtesy of WHS.)

Nine

COAL CAMP LEISURE
AND ENTERTAINMENT

Opportunities to participate in leisure activities and organized entertainment were as critical to the health and wellbeing of the residents of the coal camps as any other amenities or services. Camps with fewer opportunities tended to see higher incidences of violence and crime compared to camps with more opportunities. For this reason, coal company owners had a vested interest in providing recreational outlets for the residents of their towns.

Because the camps included not only the miners but also their families, the company needed to provide activities for all ages. Coal camp houses tended to be small, and many miners had large families. Of necessity, children spent a lot of time outside the home, visiting with friends and playing anywhere they could find a place to play. It was not uncommon for children to be allowed to go out and play so long as they were home before dark or before the streetlights came on in the camps that had them. Lacking safe play spaces, children played in the streets or sought out other places that might not be safe for play.

While the types of activities offered varied from camp to camp, every camp had some sort of outlet. These included hunting and fishing areas, bowling alleys, swimming pools, theaters, tennis courts, soda fountains, pool halls, golf courses, and social groups. Of course, all communities had informal opportunities for socialization, including house parties, barbecues, or just visiting the neighbors.

Coal companies provided services based on several criteria. Perhaps the most important was the availability of what was of interest to the local management. Secondary to that was the development of facilities the management thought would be of interest to employees that could be created with whatever limited funds were available for that purpose.

Coal miners in Floyd County had a wide range of outlets. Movie theaters, soda fountains, pool halls, swimming pools, and one golf course were all in place by the mid-1940s. Some facilities were available very early in the life of the coal camps, while others came after the camps reached maturity.

In this undated photograph, a group of teens ham it up for the camera. Pictured from left to right are Myrtle Martin, Thelma Daniels, Ted Stephens, Wilma Hayes, "Blackin" Turner, and Carolyn Proust. The Proust family had a Greek restaurant across the bridge at the end of Front Street. (Courtesy of WHS.)

Tilvus Little and two unidentified men pose in front of an early model car in this early 1930s photograph. Automobiles were luxuries in the early decades of the 20th century, even more so in the coal camps of Floyd County. Road conditions in the area at the time were primitive throughout most of the mining areas, making automobiles impractical as well as expensive to own. (Courtesy of ALC.)

The bridge in the upper photograph connects Kentucky Route 306, the only road into or out of Wheelwright, with Kentucky Route 122. Across the bridge is Wheelwright Junction. Fred Blackburn, a one-time foreman for Inland Steel, owned The Club, a combination restaurant and liquor store, and a theater here. There is also a train depot next to the theater and a Baptist church on the hill behind The Club. In the lower photograph, Mrs. Fred Blackburn works in the liquor store in The Club. Russell Lee was the photographer for these September 21, 1946 photographs. (Both courtesy of NA.)

Residents of the coal camps frequently had opportunities to engage in organized social activities. Groups for men, women, boys, and girls existed in most of the camps. In the top photograph, 10 women of the Daughters of America meet in the community hall in Wheelwright. In the lower photograph, officers of the local American Legion in Wheelwright gather for a group photograph. Both photographs were taken by Russell Lee on September 24, 1946. Other groups common in the coal camps were the Masons, the Order of the Eastern Star, Boy Scouts, Girl Scouts, and church and school groups. (Both courtesy of NA.)

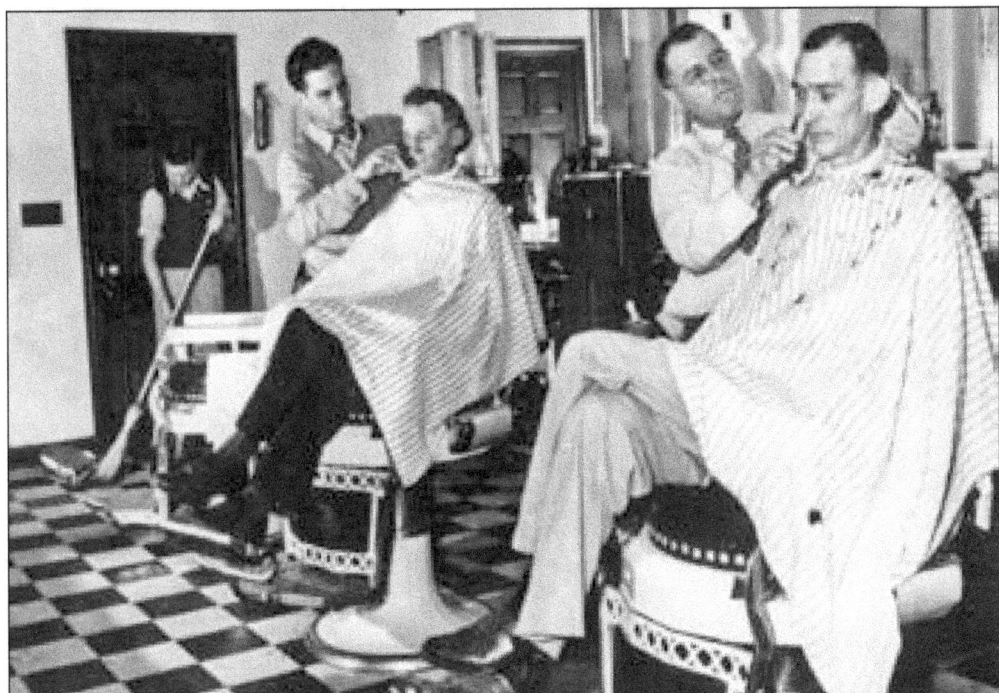

The community barbershop was not only a place for a good haircut, it also provided social opportunities for the men in the coal camps. It provided a place to discuss current happenings within the community and the world and the opportunity for exchanging ideas and engaging with others in a social setting. This photograph of the Wheelwright barbershop was taken on September 24, 1946, by Russell Lee. (Courtesy of NA.)

George Fain shows off his bowling prowess in this September 26, 1946, Russell Lee photograph. Others watch the action and wait their turn in one of the four lanes in the bowling alley in the basement of the Wheelwright Clubhouse. One job available to young men in the community was to work as pin setters in the bowling alley. (Courtesy of NA.)

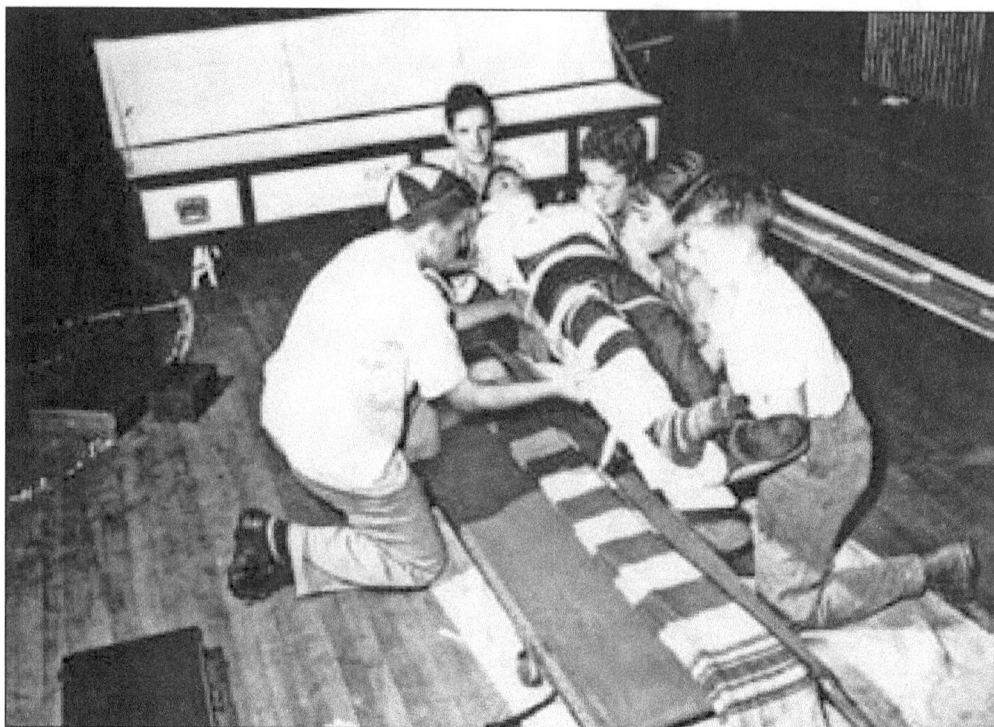

Training for mine work began early for the children in the coal camps. Here, Boy Scouts from Wheelwright practice first aid principles. Much like the safety teams in the mines, they are learning to deal with common injuries. This photograph was taken by Russell Lee on September 19, 1946. (Courtesy of NA.)

E. R. "Jack" Price (front row, left) and unidentified others gather on the stage in the school auditorium. Although the nature of the exchange is unknown, the company regularly gave away awards and other honorariums to employees for outstanding work, good safety records, and in drawings held on paydays. (Courtesy of ALC.)

About 15 people are gathered on the porch of a large wood-frame commercial building in Wheelwright. The building is unidentified but could be a boardinghouse, hotel, or company store. (Courtesy of ALC.)

Fourteen people are standing on the porch of Lee Hall Jr.'s general store in Hall Hollow in Wheelwright in 1933. His 1928 delivery truck with the name of his store is in the foreground. This privately owned store operated just a few yards outside the boundary of company property. (Courtesy of ALC.)

The Wheelwright clubhouse included a fine restaurant that served the community and visiting executives. In this photograph, a large group of people, likely management and company executives, stand outside the entrance to the hotel lobby and restaurant. (Courtesy of ALC.)

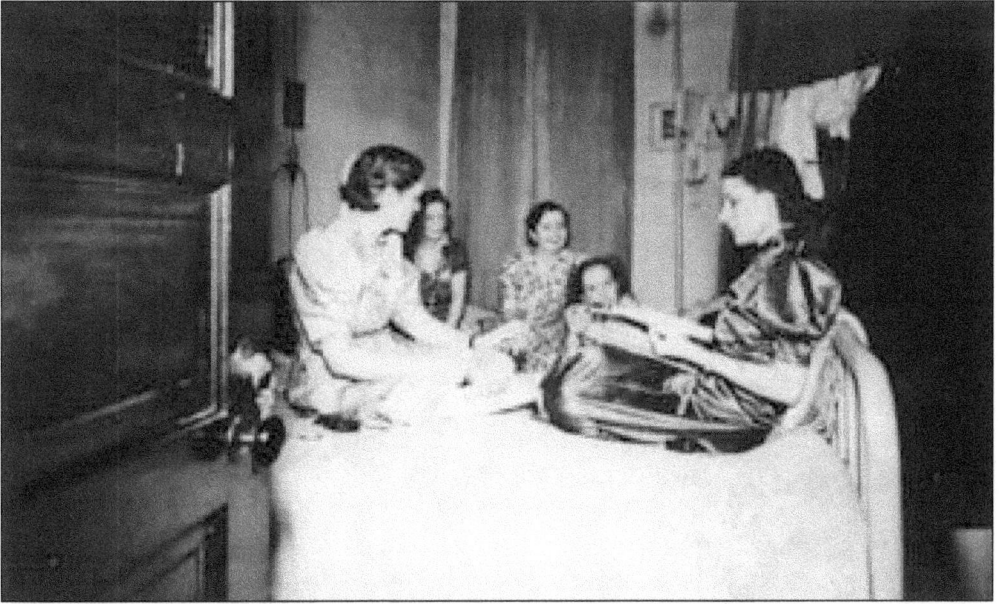

In Wheelwright, as with most other coal camps, the coal company provided lodging for single employees. This included both miners and employees in the offices, shops, hospital, construction crews, and all other jobs in the town. In these photographs, taken in the 1930s by Beecher Scutchfield, is a group of single women who worked in town. Laundry hangs to dry on a line strung across the room while the women share a magazine, a coke, and a smoke. Among these women was Scutchfield's future wife, a schoolteacher in town. Beecher Scutchfield worked in the town hospital, running the laboratory and X-ray facilities. The couple had two sons, both of whom became doctors in the Lexington area. (Both courtesy of Dr. F. Douglas Scutchfield and Dr. Scott Scutchfield.)

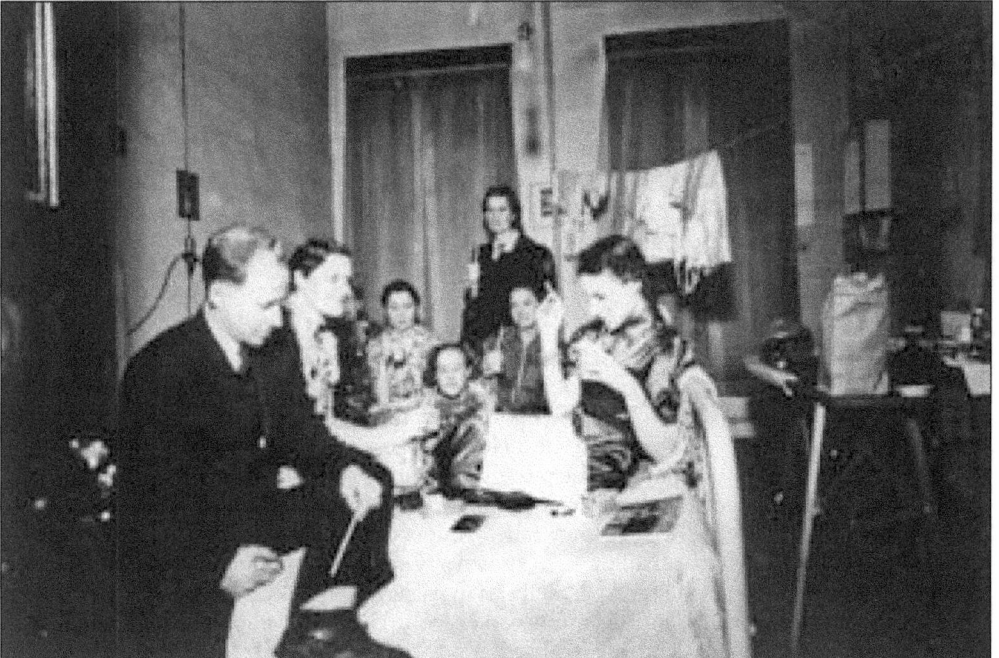

Coal companies provided different types of amenities for their employees. According to *A Medical Survey of the Bituminous Coal Industry*, a 1947 government report based on research conducted by Adm. Joel T. Boone's team conducted in the 1940s, the most common were hunting and fishing grounds and athletic facilities. Among the rarest were skating rinks, bowling alleys, gymnasiums, and golf courses. Employees of Inland Steel Company's Wheelwright mines had access to all of these rarities except a skating rink. As shown here, miners were able to spend leisure time on the company golf course in Garbage Hollow, also known as Golf Hollow or Golf Course Hollow. This nine-hole course was one of the first golf facilities in eastern Kentucky. Harry Fain's son George holds the flag while three unidentified mine workers golf. This photograph was taken by Russell Lee on September 22, 1946. (Courtesy of NA.)

Harry Fain putts as his son George holds the flag near the hole at the Wheelwright Golf Course. Note the proximity of the hillside to the putting green. The natural topography made the course a challenge both to construct and to play. The photograph, by Russell Lee, was taken on August 21, 1946. (Courtesy of NA.)

Employees of Inland Steel Company's Wheelwright mine enjoy a day on the green. Playing are C. R. Tankersley (standing on left), George Fain (standing to left of flag), Bill Wright (holding flag) and Tom Wright (child on right) along with three unidentified company employees. This photograph was taken by Russell Lee on September 21, 1946. (Courtesy of NA.)

This nice, two-story white clubhouse at the golf course on Left Otter Creek has both upstairs and downstairs porches where golfers can rest after playing on the nine-hole golf course. A few trees grow beside the clubhouse. The swimming pool and changing facility are behind the clubhouse in this 1947 picture. (Courtesy of ALC.)

This September 21, 1946, photograph provides an elevated view of the golf course at Wheelwright. Use of the golf course was available to all employees willing to pay the $16.25 annual fee the company charged for membership. A road runs parallel to the golf course, with mountains on both sides. (Courtesy of NA.)

In this view taken from the hill across Kentucky Route 306, the swimming pool and chlorine tanks are seen behind the building that houses the dressing rooms and offices for the pool. Beyond the pool lies the golf course. (Courtesy of ALC.)

Doris Stapleton poses in her swimming suit at the pool at David. She was reputed to be the best swimmer in the entire community. The latest fashion in ladies' swimwear in the 1950s was the strapless one-piece, such as Doris models here. Made in the brief style and apron style (a boy-cut to cover the upper thighs), these suits frequently used tummy support panels, boned bust support, and until well into the 1960s, a zipper in the back or the side. Two unidentified structures stand amidst the trees in the background; towels litter the ground in the foreground. (Courtesy of ALC.)

Wheelwright in the early 1940s became home to one of the first Olympic-sized swimming pools in eastern Kentucky. Presented to the executives at Inland Steel Company by E. R. "Jack" Price as a water improvement project, it quickly became a favorite summer pastime for the coal company's white families. African American miners and families were not able to use the pool in the early years. Change came after the Girl Scout troop began to offer swimming lessons to members. Although some community members disapproved of African American girls' use of the pool, the troop leader insisted the girls learn together. Their arguments helped change the policy. It was not until the late 1950s that the pool was open to all residents. (Both courtesy of NA.)

A large crowd gathers outside the Wheelwright Theater on a Saturday night. Note that workers and their families of both races are waiting in the crowd to buy tickets at the pagoda-styled ticket booth. Miners received movie passes in their pay packets at times. Although no one seems to recall there being signs or an official policy, African American moviegoers sat in the back of the theater on the right-hand side until well into the 1950s or 1960s. The ticket booth was designed by an unidentified engineering student from the University of Kentucky in Lexington. Both the theater and ticket booth were included in the 1980 National Register of Historical Places listing for Wheelwright's commercial district. (Courtesy of NA.)

Ten

LEGENDS AND HEROES

Every community has people who have contributed to the culture, development, or lore of the region. These may be businesspeople who contributed significantly to job creation, sports heroes who energized the masses, volunteers who give tirelessly of themselves to make their community better, lawmen who made people feel safe, soldiers who sacrificed their wellbeing to protect others, or ministers who shared messages of hope. They may also be infamous for bad behavior, criminal activity, or endless feuds. They are the people who give substance to the lives of others through force of will, selfless behavior, or shameless deeds; they are the source of the stories that live on long after they are gone.

Floyd County has many people who have contributed to making it a remarkable place to live. These heroes came to the county and built the towns; they left the county and made names for themselves in their chosen professions; they stayed in the county and made a difference at home. Although this chapter cannot possibly include all who have been suggested by residents around the county, those who are featured made contributions that continue to enrich the community. For them, Floyd Countians owe a tremendous debt; for those who were omitted, an equal measure of thanks is due. It is through their contributions, actions, and inspiration that the stories of the county will enrich the lives of those who are yet to come.

Billie Jean Osborne's career as a music educator in Floyd County began when she was only 17 years old; that was when she joined the faculty at Wheelwright High School as the new band director. Her contributions to music education and the conservation of traditional music in Floyd County continued as she directed band students throughout the county and later founded the Kentucky Opry in Prestonsburg. The Kentucky Opry and the Mountain Arts Center provide students in the region with music education, scholarships for children from low-income families, and cultural enrichment opportunities for the entire region. Her vision led to the founding and funding of all these programs. She continues to work to support the programs she helped to start, and her leadership will be felt by generations to come. (Portrait by Paula Goble, courtesy of Mountain Arts Center.)

118

Bert T. Combs (left, standing) held a variety of political offices in Kentucky. He was the city attorney for Prestonsburg in the 1930s and later served as governor of Kentucky from 1959 until 1963. While he was living in Prestonsburg, he established a center to provide educational opportunities for people who were, in the language of the day, mentally retarded. Among the reasons for establishing the center was that it would provide a place for his son to receive a proper education near their home. In his long career as a Democratic leader, he worked for the causes of civil rights, education, and highway construction. The Bert T. Combs Parkway serves as a major artery connecting eastern Kentucky with Interstate 64. In this late 1930s photograph, he presents a portrait of E. R. "Jack" Price, manager of the Wheelwright operations for Inland Steel Company, to Price. (Courtesy of ALC.)

"Bad" John Hall is one of the characters who will continue to live on in history. While he may never have been as bad as legend portrays him, his exploits were fodder for local news in the early 20th century. A local badman, Hall is credited with killing at least a dozen people in and around Floyd County and is rumored to have killed many more than that. In a somewhat ironic twist, Hall went on to become the local constable in Wheelwright. Although he died in 1931, the infamy of his days as a gunslinger continues to thrive in this southern Floyd County community. Many of his descendants remain in the area, and a couple will still proudly show off the guns he allegedly used in his careers on both sides of the law. In this photograph, he leans against a post holding a night stick. One gun is tucked inside his belt, while another is in his holster. (Courtesy of WHS.)

As a senior at Wayland High School in 1955, Kelly Coleman was the focal point of a lot of attention for his basketball prowess. Called "the greatest high school player who ever lived" by Adolph Rupp, the legendary basketball coach at the University of Kentucky, Coleman averaged 46.8 points per game his senior year. Recruited by many colleges and universities, "King" Kelly Coleman went on to have an outstanding career at Kentucky Wesleyan University before going on to a brief career with the New York Knicks. His success served as a shining example of how the son of a Kentucky coal miner could make a name for himself. His story continues to inspire the people of Floyd County. (Courtesy of WHS.)

Edwin R. "Jack" Price was hired by Inland Steel Company to manage its coal operations in Wheelwright shortly after it purchased the town. Under his management, the community grew from a relatively primitive coal camp into a model coal town. Among his many accomplishments in the community were infrastructure improvements such as paved streets, municipal water, and a sanitary sewer system. His leadership brought the construction of many new buildings, renovation of many older buildings, improvements in homes, and the addition of amenities such as the golf course and swimming pool. Many former residents of the camp tell stories of how Price would walk the streets daily to examine the conditions in town. If he noticed lawns in need of mowing or trash strewn about, he would demand the tenant address the problem. Miners could be forced to move out of the camp if they did not keep the property up to Price's standards. Wheelwright became known as "the town that Jack built" because of his many contributions. (Courtesy of ALC.)

Albert F. Tucker became an architect the hard way. Although his formal education ended in rural east Tennessee in the eighth grade, he worked his way up from carpenter to architect. He joined the firm of Meanor and Handloser of Huntington in 1917 and remained there until he was licensed as an architect in 1938. Shortly afterward, he was hired by Inland Steel Company to help design renovations to old buildings as well as several new buildings for the Wheelwright operation. Among his many projects in that town were the clubhouse, the community hall, the municipal building, the office building, and several others. When Wheelwright's commercial district was placed on the National Register of Historical Places in 1980, over half the buildings included in the listing were designed by Tucker. It was his interpretation of Jack Price's vision that created buildings of such lasting importance. (Courtesy of Edward Tucker Architects.)

Like small towns everywhere, the coal camps of Floyd County sent off their sons and fathers and, in some instances, their daughters and mothers, to serve their nation during times of need. Veterans memorials stand witness in many of these camps to the ones who served and the ones who died to protect their way of life. The cemeteries are filled with headstones that bear witness to their service from the Civil War to Iraq and Afghanistan. Robert Allen Triplett, a veteran of the First World War, poses in his uniform at Bevinsville about 1921. He stands here for all those who left these coalfields and for all those who were unable to return. (Courtesy of ALC.)

Finally, of all the heroes of Floyd County, perhaps the most important are all those people who grew up here, who helped to create the history of the county, and who continue to tell the stories, share the legends, and keep alive the memories because of their love of the area. Despite struggles—notably the loss of prosperity the coal boom of the early 20th century brought to the county—they continue to share the tales of one-time prosperity with anyone who will listen. They are symbolized in this photograph by a young girl and boy from the Wheelwright coal camp; without them, this story could never have been shared. They serve as a reminder that all our history is local and that it is created and preserved by those who made it. (Courtesy of Mary Lamm.)

Many African Americans came to the coalfields to work when the coal companies were opening new mines and recruiting workers. Mining in the Birmingham and Bessemer, Alabama, area was well established. African Americans in the Deep South came north looking for improved opportunities. In this 1926 photograph, approximately 30 members of the old African American church of Weeksbury stand beside a stairway at a frame building. (Courtesy of ALC.)

BIBLIOGRAPHY

Bartoletti, Susan Campbell. *Growing Up in Coal Country*. Boston: Houghton Mifflin Company, 1996.

Corbin, David Alan. *Life, Work, and Rebellion in the Coal Fields: The Southern West Virginia Miners, 1880–1922*. Urbana: University of Illinois Press, 1981.

Lewis, Ronald L. *Black Coal Miners in America: Race, Class, and Community Conflict 1780–1980*. Lexington: University Press of Kentucky, 1987.

Medical Survey of the Bituminous-Coal Industry: Report of the Coal Mines Administration. Washington, D.C.: U.S. Department of the Interior, 1947.

Report of the United States Coal Commission. Washington, D.C.: U.S. Coal Commission, 1925.

Ritch, Barbara Ford. *Coal Camp Kids: Coming Up Hard and Making It*. Tallahassee: Father and Son Publishing, 1991.

Shifflett, Crandall A. *Coal Towns: Life, Work, and Culture in Company Towns of Southern Appalachia, 1880–1960*. Knoxville: University of Tennessee Press, 1991.

Sutter, L. M. *Ball, Bat, and Bitumen: A History of Coalfield Baseball in the Appalachian South*. Jefferson, NC: McFarland and Company, 2009.

Torok, George D. *A Guide to the Historic Coal Towns of the Big Sandy River Valley*. Knoxville: University of Tennessee Press, 2004.

Weise, Robert S. *Grasping at Independence: Debt, Male Authority, and Mineral Rights in Appalachian Kentucky 1850–1915*. Knoxville: University of Tennessee Press, 2001.

ABOUT THE WHEELWRIGHT HISTORICAL SOCIETY

Wheelwright Historical Society, Inc., was founded in June 2007 by a small group of people looking to preserve the memories and heritage of Wheelwright during its days as a model coal town. It was established with three core goals: preservation of the heritage and material culture associated with Wheelwright during its years as a coal company town, advancement of educational opportunities in the region, and community development. Toward these ends, the organization has founded a volunteer-run community library that offers many special events and classes to enrich the community; established the annual Coal Camp Days Festival to raise scholarship funds for students in southern Floyd County; helped to make improvements to Peaceful Gardens, the historic African American cemetery in Wheelwright; and acquired the old coal company bathhouse, a property that is listed on the National Register of Historic Places, to restore as an educational center for the region. Funds raised through sales of this book will help to continue the work the organization has begun to enrich the area.

Because Wheelwright Historical Society is a 501(c)(3) public charity, all donations are both welcome and tax deductible. Contributions and inquiries may be addressed to:

Wheelwright Historical Society
P.O. Box 376
Wheelwright, KY 41669.

Visit us at
arcadiapublishing.com

www.ingramcontent.com/pod-product-compliance
Lightning Source LLC
Chambersburg PA
CBHW080632110426
42813CB00006B/1666